RIDERS IN THE SKY

present CLASSIC COWBOY SONGS

CONTENTS

T0057686

Shawnee Press

Exclusively Distributed By

HAL•LEONARD®
CORPORATION

7777 W. Bluemound Rd. P.O. Box 13819 Milwaukee, WI 53213

Visit Shawnee Press Online at
www.shawneepress.com

FOREWORD

In my six decades in Western Music, I've had some wonderful highs.

One of them has been knowing **Riders In The Sky** since 1986. We met over Mexican food in a café in Wichita, KS, as the boys were passing through on their way to another concert. It has turned out to be one of the blessings of my life to have known and worked with these great guys all these years. We have played shows and concerts together from the Festival of the West in Phoenix, to Carnegie Hall in New York City…And a lot of County Fairs, State Fairs, Concert Halls, Dinner Theatres, and yes, the Grand Ole Opry.

I have enjoyed every minute of being on the road with them, enjoying their great music, a lot of which is included in this songbook. I always get a thrill when they do their version of *(Ghost) Riders In The Sky*, from whence they got their name. Having lived in Wichita, KS for more than two decades, I love *Home On The Range*, which was written 100 miles from here and is a favorite of nearly everyone around the world. The great songs of the classic west, as well as those that they have created and made their own, like *That's How The Yodel Was Born*, will make for hours on entertainment as you play them and sing along with them. The guys, Ranger Doug, Too Slim, Woody Paul, and Joey the CowPolka King, are among the most talented people I have ever known, and have been crowd–pleasers every place they have played. That's why they continue to be "America's Favorite Cowboys." When I hear them do *Back In The Saddle Again* (My old boss Gene Autry's theme song) it still gives me a thrill! They are truly great artists and great men, a really hard combination to beat!

I am very fortunate that I can play their Grammy–winning recordings on my daily radio show, as I have done before I ever even met them. I know you will enjoy the great songs in this folio of the **Riders In The Sky**!

JOHNNY WESTERN AM-1070, THE RANCH, WICHITA, KS
MEMBER: COUNTRY MUSIC DISC JOCKEY HALL OF FAME
THE WESTERN MUSIC HALL OF FAME

(GHOST) RIDERS IN THE SKY
(A COWBOY LEGEND)

from RIDERS IN THE SKY

By STAN JONES

Driving and mysterious ♩ = 116 - 120

old cow-poke went rid-in' out one dark and wind-y day.
(2.) horns are black and shin-y and their hooves are made of steel.

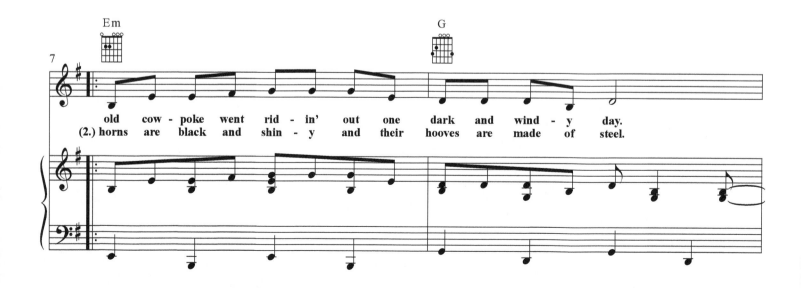

GET ALONG, LITTLE DOGIES

Traditional

THE YELLOW ROSE OF TEXAS

Words and Music by J.K., 1858

sing of Ros - a - lee,_____ But the Yel - low Rose_____ of Tex - as beats the belles_____

_____ of Ten - nes - see.

2. Where the

_____ of Ten - nes - see.

(swing 16th's)

3. Oh, I'm

spar-kle like the dew. You may talk a-bout your fair-est maid and

sing of Ros-a-lee, But the Yel-low Rose of Tex-as beats the belles of Ten-nes-see.

Yodel: Ay ee oh de loo oh lay ee, ay ee oh de loo oh lay ee, Ay ee oh de loo oh lay ee dee. Oh ay

HOME ON THE RANGE

Lyrics by Dr. BREWSTER HIGLEY
Music by DAN KELLY

THE STREETS OF LAREDO

American Cowboy Song

THAT'S HOW THE YODEL WAS BORN

Words and Music by
DOUGLAS B. GREEN

THE ARMS OF MY LOVE

Words and Music by
WOODY PAUL

trail, lead me on and I'll nev - er roam ev - er -

more from the arms of my love.

(Fiddle solo)

BACK IN THE SADDLE AGAIN

Words and Music by GENE AUTRY
and RAY WHITLEY

SWEET BETSY FROM PIKE

American Folksong

THE RED RIVER VALLEY

Traditional American Cowboy Song

HAPPY TRAILS
from the Television Series THE ROY ROGERS SHOW

Words and Music by
DALE EVANS

LONELY YUKON STARS

Words and Music by
DOUGLAS B. GREEN

(Fiddle Solo)

D.S. al Coda 𝄋

CODA

Aye ee - dle dee dee dee dee oh lo___ dee.

dee.___

rit.

rit.

(straight 8ths)